MW01265421

The Worship Continuum

GORDON MCCLURE

ISBN 978-1-0980-9002-9 (paperback)
ISBN 978-1-0980-9003-6 (digital)

Christian Faith Publishing, Inc.
832 Park Avenue
Meadville, PA 16335
www.christianfaithpublishing.com

Printed in the United States of America

FOREWORD

Isaac Smythia

If worship is an outward expression of an inner life in Christ, Pastor Gordon McClure manifests that inner life every time he picks up an instrument or opens his mouth to exalt our God. *The Worship Continuum* is an expression of the nuggets he has picked up along his journey of worship.

I have known the author for almost thirty years. Yet I found myself surprised and wanting to learn more about the transparent stories that formed Pastor Gordon as a worshipper whose goal is to lead others into the place of intimate worship.

The principles found in this book are solid and biblically based. They will help anyone who wants to worship in spirit and in truth. I would recommend using *The Worship Continuum* for training of worship leaders and teams.

ACKNOWLEDGMENTS

I think it's only right, and maybe expected, that I thank Jesus for the opportunity to write this book. After all, without Jesus, there would be no point in it. To worship Jesus is our highest calling as Christ followers. As the old song says, "All I am and ever hope to be, I owe it all to Him."

But I also think it is right that I acknowledge my beautiful worship-leading wife, Amy, my punky girl, Meagan, Liz, Sarah, and Buster the Yorkie dog. They all have given me laughs, inspiration, and encouragement in various ways about which they are probably not even aware. All are a blessing in their own way.

I must also give thanks for those who poured into me, mentored me, and shared their ministry with me in both word and action. Isaac Smythia, who came into my life and nurtured my love for missions and a desire to see people come to Jesus. Todd Braschler, who I don't call often but know he's just a phone call away to bounce ideas off of. Rick McGee, who was the guy who first encouraged me to be on a praise team back when I didn't even understand what a praise team was. Ron and Drema Webb, who instilled leadership confidence in me by hiring me to my first full-time church staff role. Larry Bradshaw, who fostered in me a love of God's Word and who would often jokingly remind me that he'd forgotten more scripture than I'd ever learned. And Dennis Wallace, who took a chance on me after a difficult time in ministry and life and saw me through the most tragic event in my life, the loss of my first wife. His love for Jesus and his love of family have inspired me for many years.

And finally to my mom, who bought that antique piano for me to learn on at age six. That's where I believe my heart for worship actually started, even though it would take years for me to become aware of it. My mom, by the way, continues to play the piano regularly at her seniors' Bible study at age eighty-seven. To all of these mentioned and to the rest of my immediate family (Dad and my brother, Steve), thank you!

INTRODUCTION

The worship continuum was born out of the urging of a few close friends that I've been fortunate enough to accumulate over the years. The idea has percolated between my ears for probably fifteen years or so. My interest in leading worship was fostered, like many worship leaders, through participation in a local church congregation's praise team. As I made a higher commitment to the team, the leader began to provide opportunities to lead after pouring into me ideas and thoughts and what might be considered a philosophy of worship.

I have been a musician since the age of six when a dear older lady would come to our home and teach me to play the piano. My mom played the piano, so this was a natural step for me. The teacher was a believer, which I didn't appreciate at the time, but would appreciate later in life. She was missing a portion of her ring finger on her right hand. It never hindered her playing as I'm sure she adapted to the missing extremity over time. As she played and taught me, she not only presented me with musical training but also a lesson about overcoming obstacles that would serve me well during challenging personal experiences that would come later in life. I progressed, did the requisite recitals, and summarily quit taking lessons after my eighth-grade year because I'd fallen in love with another instrument the summer before my eighth-grade year—the trumpet. However, the musical foundation that the piano lessons provided would serve me well throughout my life.

It was in fourth grade that I made a commitment to Christ at vacation Bible school (VBS) at a church that recently, I'm sorry to say, burned down. Oddly enough, just a few months before the church burned I spotted a picture on a friend's Facebook page of the little side building where the VBS was held that was part of my spiritual journey. The picture brought back great memories, and the church burning brought me sadness. The Sunday after I accepted Christ at that VBS I was a guest of honor at the service that morning. They brought me before the congregation to wild applause and amens. It was a reflection of what happens in heaven when the lost is found as shared in the fifteenth chapter of Luke in two of the parables found there. It was also a demonstration of their passion to see people's lives transformed by the power of Jesus. For a fourth grader, it was memorable even though somewhat overwhelming.

As I mentioned, I dropped the piano after eighth grade but later in high school was approached by some guys at school about playing keyboard in their rock band. They had been in a music theory class with me, and we seemed to connect socially and musically. I was in the high school band playing the trumpet, picking up the bass and banjo as I went along and clarifying my goal of becoming a music major in college. I knew midway through my sophomore year that I wanted to major in music in college. The offer to play in the rock band seemed to run askew of those plans in a way, but little did I know that it would be the experiences in the rock band, and many other secular bands that I'd eventually play in, that would translate so well into worship leading. Funny how God often redeems "rock and rollers" for His kingdom purposes.

As I left for college to do what I had set out to do, major in music, the freedoms of college and my mishandling of them led me down a path that would find me running away from God and ignoring His call on my life. Our middle school youth group leader had once prophesied over me that I would be a pastor, which was all I needed to hear to try and prove her wrong. I was becoming successful in all areas of music in which I participated. I was in band, orchestra, jazz band, jazz combo, and other groups all playing the trumpet. I also immersed myself in music composition writing for a variety of ensembles from "legit" to jazz. There was a semester or two that seemed like all I did was practice and rehearse six to eight hours a day. But at the same time I was playing keyboard with rock, pop, and country bands on the side in places that were clearly less encouraging of a holy lifestyle. (I even spent some time with a popular polka band that my friends would laugh about through the years. I always told them the same thing, that I laughed too—all the way to the bank.) I also began to actively write songs during these years of running from God.

All of this participation in the world of music led me not only down paths I should have never taken, but into things I deeply regret for which I've asked God's forgiveness. I reached the end of a path of depression that nearly cost me my life, yet it was in the recovery that I encountered the Holy Spirit in an incredible way that caused me to reach out for the calling God had placed on my life many years before. I confessed that I had been running from God's call, that I was a jerk to others because my main goal was self-promotion, and that I wanted to be more famous than Jesus. It was at that point that I decided it was God's desire that I make Jesus more famous than me. In short, I surrendered to God. It's then that doors began to open that led me into worship leading.

Over time the Lord would place various mentors in my life, some of them keenly aware that they were pouring into me and others unwittingly doing so. As I look back at my life I can now see the role that each of them played in discipling me. All of us should be so fortunate to have many people who mentor, encourage, and pour into us asking for nothing in return except that God be high and lifted up in our life. I also believe we should be mentoring others as we go along in our journey. Over time I served on praise teams playing both trumpet and piano/keyboard, invited the Holy Spirit to lead me as I led others, and served as a worship leader at churches in Ohio, Illinois, Colorado, and Kansas. Each church was a special blessing, and it was an honor to serve each congregation. I began to hone my current understanding of what it means to seek the anointing each time I lead worship.

So the idea for this book landed somewhere between Colorado and Kansas some fifteen years ago. It was put on the shelf when my first wife passed away unexpectedly leaving me with a beautiful daughter to raise alone. She was six years old at the time of her mother's passing. But "the worship continuum" idea has been resurrected now after being married again to, of all things, a worship leader. When I think of my "new family," a blended family, I'm thankful that God's faithfulness never abandoned me and that I now trust His timing in the writing of this book. My hope is it will be an encouragement to others in worship ministry. Please understand, I'm not a *famous* worship leader. I'm just a guy who finds a particular blessing in blessing God through worship. I hit just as many wrong notes as the next person, but I like to think that I do so out of a passion for Jesus and seeing Him transform lives.

The idea of the worship continuum is actually very simple. When we worship, we are joining our voices with the voices who've praised God in ages past, who are worshiping Him right now, and joining our voices with those who will worship Him in the future. When we worship, we join our voices with the worship that's taking place in heaven this very moment. It's a worship that has always existed and never ceases. It's a continuum of worship that has no beginning and will have no end.

It's my hope that you'll enjoy reading *The Worship Continuum* and that it will be meaningful in some way so as to encourage you in your worship lifestyle. If you're a worship leader or on a worship team, I particularly hope that it will open your eyes to the sacred role of what you do week in and week out as you serve at your church faithfully. God sees you, my friend, and He loves you and your heart of worship!

CHAPTER 1

Heavenly Worship
Leader Gone Wrong

The Ego Trap

We have to first acknowledge a terrible truth. The devil was the main worship leader in heaven. If we don't recognize this, we'll never fully understand the role that worship plays in spiritual warfare. If we don't recognize this, we can get easily trapped in that same trap of ego and pride that caused Satan to be ejected from heaven along with his minions.

We will only worship something that we believe is greater than we are. The enemy aspired to be equal to God and, in doing so, fractured his role as a worship leader leading to his dismissal. Ego and pride are still knocking at the door of our hearts and in some ways maybe more at the hearts of worship leaders. The enemy understands the power of our praise, and he's at odds with it. If he can trip us up, get our focus on self, and encourage our ego, then we begin to fall for his deceptions.

Make no mistake, as worship leaders we must regularly examine our motives and confess our wrong motives to the object of our worship, Jesus. Sometimes this is easier said than done. Who doesn't enjoy a good compliment after leading worship? It's human nature to enjoy them, and if your love language is words of affirmation

11

you have to be especially careful. This is why an understanding of the worship continuum is so important. To see worship as ongoing, never ceasing, and not an event is important to helping us curb our egos and put things into perspective.

If we find our identity in any other person or thing than Jesus, we run the risk of feeling entitled to the compliments and accolades with which the enemy deceives us at times. Now I'm not saying that we should totally shun a good attaboy or attagirl. It's about what our hearts do with it. Sooner or later we can become dependent upon those flattering words. As the compliments dry up, so does our passion for worship. This ought not be! Our passion for worship should be as consistent as God Himself and rooted in our desire to bless God with the incense of our praise.

To this end I encourage you not to feign humility when the compliments come, but rather find a trusted brother or sister in Christ who will be real with you. A person who's not afraid to be honest with you, one who'll remind you of the fleshly odor that arises when we begin to think higher of ourselves than we should, one who will tell you when you've genuinely connected people to the heart of God through your leading.

Awareness, Not Fear

Now back for a moment to the spiritual warfare part of this essay. I tell those I lead that *we need not live in fear of the enemy, but we should live in awareness of him.* To deny his existence is to open the door to him. Jesus, in the New Testament, encountered the enemy when He was being tempted in the desert (Matthew 4:1–11). He cast out demons in His earthly ministry (and still does today in His heavenly ministry). He speaks to the disciples about the enemy, and the enemy even asked to "sift" Peter like wheat (Luke 22:31–32). The enemy's goal is to kill and destroy and deceive in ways that will lead us away from Jesus and not toward Him. He is naturally inclined to be in opposition to our worship of God.

Because there is an enemy of which we are aware, we need to cultivate a rich prayer life. Worship and prayer go hand in hand. They're often paired together for powerful ministry to God and people. In many ways, to have a heart of worship is to have a heart of prayer. I'm of the mind that one without the other falls short of God's best design for both. If you're a leader of a team, please make praying together a regular part of your gathering and rehearsals. Insist that those on your team cultivate their prayer life and individual worship life (I'll talk more about that in a later chapter). We're blessed to live in a time where there are many resources available to help us cultivate prayer as a way of life.

I had the honor of ministering in Uruguay, South America, several years ago. I recall a time in the town of Rocha where I was preaching at a revival in the town plaza. The lighting was such that it created a clear, circular perimeter that dropped off immediately into darkness. As we began ministering that evening I noticed there were few people sitting in the lighted area. However, I would look out to the dark area from time to time and notice small, red lights appearing then rising, then dropping and disappearing again. I was baffled and frankly somewhat concerned about what it could be. I later realized that it was people raising lit cigarettes to their lips then dropping them down until the next drag. There were bunches of people sitting out there concealed in the dark hearing our message of freedom in Christ.

Now I'm not sharing this to make a statement about whether Christians can smoke and still be saved, but rather I want us to see from this illustration that there is dark and there is light in the spiritual realm. The good news is that worship can be used to influence those walking in the dark to come into the light of Jesus! Some received Christ at that crusade, and some were delivered from demonic possession. It was a time that we could have easily given into the fear of the enemy, but God had bigger plans for those services! Worship was part of the setting free of people and the battle against the enemy's strongholds in people's lives.

13

Jumpin' Jehoshaphat

I love teaching on the passage in 2 Chronicles 20 and could probably write a book just about this chapter, but perhaps I'll save that for another time. For now, I'd like to give a condensed version of the miracle of worship that took place.

Jehoshaphat was a king of Israel who took the throne at age thirty-five, and it was during his twenty-five-year reign that the account in chapter 20 takes place. Jehoshaphat is confronted with the truth that several groups had come to make war with him and Israel. We see a progression that shows us a glimpse of his heart as he humbles himself not only before God, but before his people. He confesses that he doesn't have a clue about what to do. I've felt that way many times in my life. What he said next is so meaningful. He declared that his eyes were on God despite his lack of knowing what to do. It's an expression of complete dependence upon our Creator.

What happens next is a Pentecostal's dream (of which I'm one). The Holy Spirit descended on Jahaziel, and a powerful Word from the Lord came forth to the king and the people—verse 15 says, "Do not be afraid or discouraged because of this vast army. For the battle is not yours, but God's." He followed this up with specific insight into how the enemies would attack the army of Israel. Upon hearing this Word through Jahaziel, the king bowed before his people to honor God and the people followed suit. Next, loud praise came from a group of Levites!

But this isn't the best part. No doubt God's assurance to not be afraid and to trust Him was comforting, but then the king consulted some of his key leaders and they came to a conclusion that doesn't make much sense in the natural, but in the spiritual there's a lesson for us to learn. He called for the singers to go out at the head of the army. Read it for yourself in your Bible. I ask you, would you pick the choir to be the first ones to engage a powerful enemy in battle? Not likely. Nothing against choirs. I've known some burly men in the choirs that I've led over the years that I'd prefer go before me in battle, but what the choir did was sing praises to God.

They didn't just sing, but they were the catalyst for the complete annihilation of the opposing armies! The choir's praise caused God's hand to move against the opposing armies making them turn on each other and destroy each other. No arrows of the king's army were shot, no spears were thrown, no swords were drawn! All that was left to do was collect the plunder, which no doubt fortified their weapons stockpile, contributed to their treasury, and filled their bellies with food. When we worship, something happens in the heavenlies and our enemy can be defeated by God's power.

Interesting sideline about Jahaziel: one of his ancestors was a guy named Asaph. Look no further than the Psalms to find his name as one of the writers. He also led the worship before the ark of the covenant when it was brought back to Jerusalem during King David's reign.

To lead in worship and to join in *the worship continuum* is spiritual. It's warfare. It's powerful. It's sacred. It can be supernatural.

CHAPTER 2

<hr />

When Heaven Meets Earth

Asuza Street and the Heavenly Chorus

It's hard to understand at times that two realms exist at the same time. One is temporal or natural, and the other spiritual. As Christians we understand that what we do in the natural realm can affect that which is in the spiritual realm, and vice versa. Prayer is something we do in the natural, which impacts the spiritual and, when guided by the Holy Spirit, brings the best of both realms together in many ways. When the spiritual realm manifests itself in the natural realm, we usually call this supernatural. I truly believe that it's worship that can foster the meeting, the comingling of these two realms giving us glimpses of the eternity we'll one day live with Christ.

In the early years of the twentieth century a man named William Seymour received ministry and spiritual training at a school in Topeka, Kansas, not too far from where I currently live. His instructor was a man named Charles Parham. There are no doubt more detailed ways to share Seymour's story, but for the purposes of understanding the worship continuum I'll give a more brief account.

Seymour traveled to Los Angeles, California, to establish a church. Like many church start-ups, his church was fostered in his home with a few close friends and a lot of prayer. No doubt worship was also part of the picture. As Seymour identified the need to have a meeting place for a larger crowd, he was able to secure a humble setting for the purposes of gathering for worship, prayer, and teaching of the Word. This building was located in Azusa Street, and the revival that rose out of it would come to be known as the Azusa Street Revival. Several present-day Pentecostal denominations and voluntary cooperative fellowships have their roots in the Azusa Street Revival.

There are accounts given by eyewitnesses, or maybe we should actually say "ear witnesses." As the people worshiped vigorously, additional voices were heard that joined in the celebration. These voices weren't from people in the room in the natural realm, but rather believed to be the voices of angels who were worshiping with the believers in the spiritual realm. The natural realm collided with the spiritual realm, or the spiritual realm collided with the natural. No matter what you want to call it, it was supernatural. These voices came to be commonly known as "the heavenly chorus." It appears it wasn't just a one-time occurrence either. It was a phenomenon. It was supernatural. It was a picture of the worship continuum that joins our voices with the voices of the angels worshiping around the throne of God day and night.

Angels around the Throne

Is there some kind of explanation for this incredible convergence of earth and heaven? It seems reasonable if you consider that there are angels who worship God around His Throne day and night and that God does permit glimpses into heaven through His Word and supernaturally. There are even accounts of people clinically dying and going to heaven only to be revived and return with vivid descriptions of what they saw. Some of these accounts have even been made into movies.

There are several primary texts in Scripture that point to the continual worship of God by angels around His throne. We see in the early verses of Isaiah 6 a picture of worship by the angels as they gathered around the throne of God. They declared the Lord holy and pronounced that He is omnipotent or almighty. It's a picture of loud praise that emphasizes the holiness of God.

We see a representation of the Isaiah 6 passage brought forward into chapter 4 of the book of Revelation, a literal quote of the Isaiah 6 passage. We keep reading into verses 9 to 10 and see that the twenty-four elders joined in the worship as they laid down their crowns at the throne of God and declared Him as Creator of all things.

Fast-forward to chapter 5 of the book of Revelation and we see the description of similar images with the addition of harps as the angels and elders worship Jesus, the Lamb who was slain. In this passage we see the worthiness of God declared.

Go backward in time and we see that in 1 Kings 22 the obscure prophet Micaiah, who was at odds with King Ahab, gave a description of a gathering around God's throne. Further study of this section of Old Testament scripture reveals that King Ahab took issue with Micaiah because he never prophesied anything in the king's favor. In fact, it took Jehoshaphat to convince Ahab to even consider listening to Micaiah. Turns out that of all the prophets that Ahab consulted on this particular matter, Micaiah was the only one who got it right. That correct prophecy included the death of King Ahab.

Though none of these accounts specifically indicates that music was used in the worship around the throne, there are hints that there was music because some of these passages talk of harps in the hands of the angels. One can presume that since angels were noted in Scripture to sing at times that singing was likely part of the worship. Even if it wasn't, the main thing that is happening at God's throne is worship of some kind. Bowing, declaring God's worthiness to be praised, declaring of God's holiness, a reminder that worship isn't always connected to music.

Heaven Touched Us That Night

In 2011 I had the opportunity to return to South America just two years after my wife had passed away. It was on my previous trip in 2009 that I received word on our return trip from Uruguay in the

Dallas airport that my wife had unexpectedly died. This was on the heels of a tremendous time of ministry throughout the country. Our church had put together a praise team to travel to Uruguay to do sort of a mini-tour of the country where we held evangelistic services in various places including a teen challenge center in Montevideo. (Teen challenge centers can be found throughout the world, and they do amazing work and ministry with recovering addicts.) It was a rich time of ministering through worship music, the Word, and altar ministry praying for hundreds of people over the course of our time there. I'll share more in chapter 5 about the role that worship played in my healing from my wife's passing.

We were invited back to be a guest praise team at a 2011 youth camp, which gathered youth and their families from all over the country. I was asked to share some teaching sessions on worship in addition to our band leading worship at various times over the course of the camp. It was a powerful time of ministry that not only afforded us the privilege of ministering to others but also a personal time of healing for me.

After a week or so of great preaching and worship, we arrived at the closing night of the camp. There were other praise teams there from various parts of South America including Peru and Uruguay. As one of the praise teams was leading after the guest speaker that evening, something supernatural happened that was what I believe today to be the closest I've come in my life, so far, to experiencing the "heavenly chorus."

The Holy Spirit began to manifest Himself through the people's singing in a unique way. Our team was backstage listening and trying to come to grips with what was going on. It was clear it was of God, and one of my ministry partners was able to grab his digital sound recorder and began recording a small portion of the sound that we were hearing. Though the sound of what was going on was over-whelming, it didn't quite capture the entire experience. The Holy Spirit would move in waves of sound and presence as the people worshipped. The volume and intensity of people's praise would rise and fall, and I felt like I was riding in a small boat being lifted up on top of the wave then smoothly sailing down to the trough of the wave, up again then down, up again then down. The cycle continued as the Holy Spirit ministered to people, and they responded in singing, shouting, bowing, jumping, clapping. It was a Holy Spirit party like I've never seen or heard. My description of the event falls short of actually having witnessed it firsthand. I have a small audio clip of that evening's move of God that I cherish and hope I never misplace. Even if I do, the memory is indelibly etched on my mind and heart. I believe I heard the voices of heaven join with ours that warm evening in Uruguay. It was a taste of heaven on earth.

We were part of the worship continuum, and it's been my desire to experience this sort of thing again though I'd be content to have experienced it only once this side of heaven. It wasn't something that could be manufactured or manipulated. It was just something that the Holy Spirit did as hundreds came before God to worship Him humbly with reverence and awe.

CHAPTER 3

<><><><><><><><><><><><><><><><><><><><><><><><><><><><><><><><><><><><><>

Strange Fire

Reverence and Awe

I've dialogued with fellow worship leaders over the years about the merit of my statement that there is a *right* way to worship rooted in holiness. There is *strange fire* that can be offered up before the Lord as we lead worship when we allow the flesh or a spirit of performance to enter into the worship setting. There are spiritual consequences for offering strange fire. It's my belief that we must always be on guard of our hearts being focused on first leading ourselves into God's presence then inviting people to go on this worship journey with us (Leviticus 10:1).

This is where I would challenge anyone reading this manifesto of sorts to consider their motivation for being on a praise team whether you're the appointed leader or not. I believe that if you're on a praise team, no matter your instrumental or vocal role, you *are* a worship leader though we typically designate some to lead the group. If you're on the team, then you're a lead worshiper. Your responsibility to be spiritually prepared is just as important as the person *out front* who may be leading the song. You individually bring with you stuff to the platform. (I use the word *platform* because I have an aversion to the word *stage* as I believe it fosters an idea of performance.)

When I say that we bring our *stuff* to the platform, I'm not asserting that we have to be perfect to be on the platform in a worship role. If that were the case, none of us would be on the platform at all. Only Jesus is perfect. However, we should, as worship team members, be always in pursuit of becoming more like Jesus. My theological foundations are Wesleyan, so I hold to the belief that as people who've accepted Jesus as Savior that sanctifying grace is at work in us. That grace carries us along in our Jesus journey as we become honed by the Holy Spirit to become more and more like Jesus. In other words, we're growing in Christ to be more like Him. As those who lead worship we should always be seeking to grow in our understanding of the person of Jesus and applying it to our lives. This will impact the way we lead worship and our ability to bring people with us into God's presence.

Our Lifestyle Does Matter

There are two factors that play into my "lifestyle matters" thought. One is the lifestyle that people see in public, and the other is our private lifestyle. They should be consistent with each other, yet sometimes aren't. Because worship ministry in a local church setting is so public and visible in nature, people tend to recognize you among the body of believers and in the general public. It's just the nature of being up in front of people on a regular basis. If you're in a large church setting, it's pretty likely people who you don't know most definitely know who you are. This is simply part of the role.

If you have struggles in your private life, great discernment is necessary to know how to navigate those struggles. Back to an earlier point, avoiding offering strange fire doesn't mean your perfect. How you handle your struggles, however, is important. The challenge of being consistent in both arenas, public and private, is an ongoing one. If you have personal struggles, hidden sin, unholy habits, then I implore you get help from a trusted friend or, if needed, a professional. It's so vital to have an accountability system in place with trusted friends or at least one accountability partner who's willing to hold you to a standard of holiness. We all need accountability, and when practiced with grace and love, the church community is the best place for it.

In a recent sermon series written by my church's youth pastor, he developed preaching outlines that centered on how the church is to live in contrast to a post-modern mind-set that permeates our culture. I believe this is true and that especially as worship leaders and Christ followers we should live biblically and not culturally. There should be a distinction between how we live our lives and how culture says we should. The dependence on self that our culture cultivates, the self-focused lifestyle, and other factors can push us to develop our own truths that run contrary to the truth of God's Word. It's not easy with cultural factors pressing in on us, but for our eternity's sake we ought to live according to God's truth and not the world's. I call this "Big T" living as opposed to "small t" living.

I recall a time that I had a drummer in a praise team several years ago who had a particular bad habit from which he was seeking freedom. I counseled with the man, and he wanted to be set free; he simply hadn't achieved it yet. It was something that he felt kept him from a deeper relationship with God and something he felt was a stumbling block to others. I appreciated his honesty with me, and I could tell he was somewhat uncomfortable sharing his struggle with me. He had the fear of being kicked off of the praise team.

As I listened to him I discerned he was sincere in his efforts to overcome the struggle. It was a struggle that I didn't personally consider a moral issue because Scripture doesn't speak specifically to his habit. If I had felt it was a moral issue, I would have handled it all differently and have had to at times with moral issues among musicians on teams I led. I told him I'd stand in accountability with him, pray for him, and put into place a plan to rid himself of the unhealthy habit. He overcame the issue in a matter of weeks. I'm confident that if I had kicked him off of the team at that time that he would continue to struggle with it. I was willing to lose an unrepentant and talented drummer over a moral issue, but this fellow's sincerity of wanting to overcome the issue so he could have a deeper relationship with Jesus meant that he would ultimately also benefit from a worship standpoint. His playing improved dramatically once the burden of his challenge was lifted, and he was set free. I believe he achieved his desire to have a deeper relationship with Jesus, and it shone through in his worship. Drummers can truly worship, by the way.

Commitment Is a Spiritual Issue

I served many years under the spiritual authority of a pastor who would often encourage the staff with a phrase that is actually the name of a classic devotional book by Oswald Chambers. We'd be in a staff meeting, and he would discern that someone was wanting to give less than their best to a project or task and would say, "My utmost for His highest." What he was telling us was that the project or task was worth our highest commitment because it was for kingdom purposes. The phrase redirected us. It brought us into focus. That phrase comes to mind when I become weary and look for an easy way out of something that truly deserves my best effort and personal resources. Ministry deserves our greatest effort and talent applied to it. There are souls at stake and eternities to be chosen by people. Not so much eternities but rather the destination of each person's eternity. Simply put, God deserves our best.

Another mentor of mine who was a denominational leader who oversaw the worship ministry of the denomination once told me, "Commitment is a spiritual issue." It is from his statement that I take my cue for this section of this chapter. Being on a praise team requires commitment. It requires both individual preparation and group preparation. It requires a deep relationship with Christ and a commitment to lead people into God's presence in worship. To approach it casually relegates it to simply playing through a list of songs. Worse yet is just playing through a list of songs then leaving the service and not even hearing the message for which our worship has tilled the soil of people's hearts.

I think it speaks loudly of a praise team's spiritual commitment to be in unity with the person preaching in a service when they either stay in the service or, at the very least, observe it from a monitor in

some location. I was on a praise team once where we had two moni-
tors behind the platform so we could hear the message and come out
at the appropriate time in order to create a smooth transition. I've
also been on teams where the praise team got up from their seats in
the worship space at the appropriate time and made their way to the
platform. The *how* of it all isn't as important as the *why*. Praise teams
need to see their role in the service as one of the worship elements
and not the only worship element. In a worship service everything is
a part of worship from the music, to the offering, to the praying, to
the responses, to the message from God's Word, etc. Spiritual unity
of all involved in a service creates a truly God-honoring and God-
focused service. If you are of the mind that your role on a praise team
is just to play songs, then leave the service. I'd encourage you to assess
your heart's motives. You may be offering strange fire before the Lord
and creating spiritual risk for your team.

CHAPTER 4

Golden Altar of Incense

The Tabernacle Progression

Those who have been around me for any length of time have probably heard me bounce around the term *tabernacle progression*. I don't know if this is an original expression or one that has been used by others. I just know it's my way of expressing that leading a group in worship requires us to take them somewhere. Therefore, there is a progression of some sort that takes us from point A to point B. It's not intended to be formulaic as there are times that the worship-leading situation calls for a different approach. At other times, the Holy Spirit might lead in a different direction in the middle of a planned worship set, and this sort of goes out the window. However, by and large, a concept of the tabernacle progression has served me well as a worship leader and as a person who desires to foster a lifestyle of worship.

We trace an understanding of the tabernacle progression back to the exodus of the Israelites from Egypt. The reason Moses gave Pharaoh for the Israelites leaving Egypt is often overlooked. It was to worship their God. As the saga of the exodus unfolds Moses encounters God in a profound way during which God gives Moses the very specific plans for the tabernacle or place of worship (Exodus 26–30). It was a detailed description of the tabernacle that required the people to give an offering. By the way, the offering that was given was so large that eventually Moses had to tell the people to stop giving (Exodus 36:2–7). With the resources of the people, the instructions for the creation of the tabernacle, and the guidance of God, the tabernacle was completed and became the center of worship for the Israelites. On the day that the tabernacle was opened for business, so to speak, God manifested His presence in a mighty way (Exodus 40:34–38).

Thus began the ministry of the Levites whose service centered around the tabernacle. Each Levite had a role and function in the life of the tabernacle, which carried over into the worship roles at the temple in Jerusalem generations later. As worship leaders we ought to consider ourselves modern-day Levites who have a specific role in the *temple* or our place of worship. It's a sacred role that is centuries old.

An in-depth study of the tabernacle is something the reader should consider, but for the purposes of this book a simple overview will suffice. Though there is a lot to be gained by learning more about the details of the tabernacle and the various roles the Levites played, I'll leave that to you, the reader, to pursue on your own. There are many fine resources for that kind of study.

The tabernacle was a mobile structure which complimented the nomadic lifestyle of the Israelites at that time. Later in the history of Israel a temple would be built in Jerusalem as a more permanent structure even though it would be destroyed and rebuilt a number of times. Nonetheless, the tabernacle and the temple had this in common. There were three distinct sections: the outer court, the holy place, and the holy of holies.

The outer court was the place were animals were brought by the Israelites to be offered as sacrifices. There is a rich meaning behind the various reasons for sacrifice that can also be studied in depth as it gives even more significance to the sacrifice Jesus made on the cross. The outer court had a group of priests that would serve the people as they brought their animals to be sacrificed. Some of the priests would slaughter the animals for sacrifice, others would wash the parts, and others would burn them. There was a laver, a type of washbasin, for cleansing and a burnt altar. This is a simplistic overview of their roles which leads me to share that the outer court was a loud and active place. Just imagine the animals being brought in for slaughter, the people talking, the priests giving direction, etc. Yet it was the first part of the tabernacle progression which would ultimately lead to the manifested presence of God.

When our people gather to worship, in a sense, they come with an outer court mind-set. Many come prepared to worship, however, the time before a service begins is typically filled with talking, laughter, noisiness of different kinds. The motives of people's hearts are usually quite varied from the person eager to worship to the person who's only there because Mom or Dad dragged them to church. Still others, and we can never forget this, are there because they're exploring and searching. This is where the role of the worship leader begins to bring people from the outer court to the next section of the tabernacle and it's vital.

Typically I'll start off with an upbeat song that invites people to join in with singing, clapping, moving of some kind, even dancing. It's something that signals we've begun taking steps towards more recognition of God's presence. God is omnipresent so our task is to help people recognize His presence more deeply. It creates a type of celebration that draws people into a direction, hopefully the same direction. Then after a series of songs and time we move to the holy place.

The holy place was a place where several higher echelon priests would serve. There were three things in the holy place: the table of shewbread, the golden lampstand that was to remain lit at all times, and the golden altar of incense. An in-depth study of all three of these items is worth your while, but we'll not delve into that here. I would only say that there is great symbolism in each.

This space was more solemn in contrast to the outer court. It was not noisy and calamitous like the outer court. Only priests were allowed in, and even then, they were select priests with specific duties. It was a holy place but not the holiest. That was to come next after lingering in the holy place for a bit.

When leading worship I tend to think of songs that are medium in tempo, maybe slower, certainly slower than the outer court songs. These are songs that tend to change our focus from we to me or from us to Him. Our heart begins to shift toward the face of God that we'll encounter in the next section of the tabernacle.

The golden altar of incense was up near the curtain that separated the holy place from the holy of holies. There was also a curtain that separated the outer court from the holy place. These curtains help distinguish the three sections of the tabernacle.

You may have heard the expression "the incense of our worship." That expression is most often a reference to the golden altar of incense, which would have been producing smoke from the burning of incense and a pleasing aroma. In my mind, as I worship, I'm creating a pleasing aroma of incense that rises up to God. It's a place of preparation to meet with Him face-to-face in a manner of speaking. I'm preparing my heart to encounter my Creator. I leave my ego and self-focus behind abandoned for the sake of encountering God face-to-face.

Our hearts are ready. The aroma of our worship is billowing from the altar of our heart that is burning incense to God. Then we step into the holy of holies—the very presence of God! In the holy of holies is the ark of the covenant. On top is what is known as the mercy seat, two angels with wings extended toward each other as they bow down. It's a great image of the posture of our heart and perhaps the posture of our bodies when we reach this point in the tabernacle progression. A place of submission and awe!

Inside the ark of the covenant were significant icons for the Israelites. The ark of the covenant was taken before the armies of Israel many times in battle. Many times the Israelites would miraculously win battles in which the odds appeared against them. As word spread through the region, other armies began to recognize the power of the ark of the covenant and even attributed its power to the God of the Israelites. As with many things over time, the power of the ark began to be taken for granted and was eventually captured by the archenemy of Israel, the Philistines. The ark was eventually returned to Israel, but only after God afflicted the Philistines with rats and hemorrhoids. Many versions of the Bible use the word *tumors* for hemorrhoids, however, that is not an accurate translation of what was really going on (1 Samuel 5–6). It was King David who arranged the procession that would bring the ark of covenant to the temple in Jerusalem.

Inside the ark were three things: Aaron's rod that budded, a pot of manna, and the Ten Commandments (Hebrews 9:3–5). All of these icons were testament to God's power and presence among the Israelites before the tabernacle was constructed.

Now we're in the holy of holies, the presence of God, and the songs we sing turn from self to God. Slow, worshipful utterances from the heart like Jesus, God, You, Holy Spirit, lover of my soul, giver of life, perhaps attributes of God, and the list could go on. The focus is never on us but rather only on God, the object of our worship. We bow, we weep, we may even remain silent. But not matter our expression we've arrived at the goal of our worship, to be in the presence of God and honor Him with our worship! It's here that God can transform us, speak to us, lavish His love on us in even greater ways.

I tell people we should never come to worship in order to receive something. We come only to give, to give to our Master. But, in the giving of ourselves to Him, there is always a reciprocation. We come into His presence to give our worship and praise, but we leave with hearts full and transformed having received from God. There's a great exchange that takes place. We sometimes come with our hurt and pain and leave with healing and encouragement for having spent time at the Master's feet. There's simply no place like God's presence, and as worship leaders, like the Levites, we have a sacred role to lead and guide people to the holy of holies. We help people create and maintain their reverence and awe of God's presence.

Go There before Them

Can I tell you something that transformed my worship leading that I learned from a mentor years ago? It seems so simple yet requires commitment and discipline in some ways. Here it is. *We can't take people in worship any farther than we've been ourselves.* There's a difference in worship when the worship leader is not in strange territory. There's a type of holy confidence in the worship leader because they know how to get there. That's not to say that people who don't lead worship don't know how to get there. After all, we must first fundamentally lead ourselves in our faith, in spiritual disciplines, and in worship. But a person who's leading worship that has never really been in God's presence is just leading through a list of songs. As a worship leader you can never relegate your times of worship to Sunday morning when you're leading. *You have to know the way before you take the group with you.*

My family traveled to New York City about a year ago to visit one of my and Amy's daughters who had just made it into her first Broadway production. It was a proud-parent moment for us. Our youngest daughter travelled with us, and none of the three of us had ever been in NYC. We'd read about it, we'd seen pictures, we'd watched movies shot in NYC, but we'd never experienced it for ourselves. In many ways it was overwhelming, and in other ways it was like watching a great sociological experiment. We had a great time!

Since we had never been there we relied on people to help us navigate. First, it was the cab driver who took us from the airport to our motel near Times Square. His knowledge of the city was hugely valuable. Then we relied on the doorman at the motel to give us insight as to the best restaurants and their locations. Then we really stepped out of our comfort zone and purposed to ride the subway to Harlem where our daughter's apartment was so we could have breakfast together. It was because of her experience on the subway and her expert instructions that we made it there on time with our dignity intact. My point? They all knew how to get where we wanted to go. Without them, we would have wondered around aimlessly, reliant upon our lack of experience in NYC. It could have and likely would have been disastrous!

Worship leaders, the deeper you go in worship personally, the deeper those you lead will go. You have a sacred responsibility. You are a Levite in modern times.

CHAPTER 5

≈≈

Leading from a Place of God's Presence

The Torn Veil

There is no more important scripture to me as a worship leader than the passage that's found in all of the Gospels, except for John, in regards to the veil or curtain in the temple at the time of Jesus's death (Matthew 27:51, Mark 15:38, Luke 23:45). These specific verses describe a moment that God supernaturally coordinated activity between the cross and the temple—a moment that would rock the Passover celebration.

Jesus on the cross "gave up the ghost," as the King James Version of the Bible says and, at the precise moment, the veil in temple that separated the holy place from the holy of holies was ripped from top to bottom exposing the holy place for people to see. It was a definitive work that symbolizes to us today the privilege we have to go into God's presence at any time without ritual or animal sacrifice! What a picture of liberation! No more need for a priest to gain access to God Himself. We can come boldly with humility into God's presence. What a gift to His people (Hebrews 4:16)!

When we lead worship we're inviting people to journey into a place that was once forbidden that is now a place which is completely accessible. That's an amazing contrast. I praise God for this miraculous act almost as much as the act that was taking place over on Calvary's hill as Jesus died for my sins. Praise God for the shed blood of Christ and praise God for the torn veil!

In My Darkest Hour

There was a season of my life over a decade ago that in some ways forced me to live dependent on God's presence. It was a time that required great faith, it was a time of testing, and in the end it turned out to be a time of tragedy. I sat in the Dallas airport with a group of worship leaders who had gone to minister in Uruguay, South America. Through a close and treasured relationship with a missionary friend, I'd arranged to bring a team of musicians to travel throughout the country to conduct services. It was a wonderful time of ministry and a time of bonding with this group of brothers in Christ.

As we rested from our long journey awaiting the final flight home, one of the members of the band got a phone call. I noticed the expression on his faced seemed puzzled. He walked over to me and handed me the phone telling me it was our pastor and he wanted to talk to me. The pastor on the other end wasn't just my pastor, but a close friend as well. He shared through a cracking voice that my wife had been found deceased. This close friend and others on the trip had been walking with me through the journey of addiction that had now claimed my wife's life.

Years earlier she had been in a terrible car accident, which left her in continual and debilitating pain. She had become addicted to prescription pain medications long before the current awareness of the opioid crisis in America. Our precious daughter had been born in the midst of this season of addiction. The scenario drove me to my knees daily, sometimes multiple times a day. The need to be in God's presence was not just a luxury but a necessity, and I would learn to never take His presence for granted.

During the years leading up to this tragedy I had come to a place of realizing that so much was out of my control. I had surrendered my heart to being a person of God's presence striving to not let my circumstance dictate my worship. I was not perfect. I made mistakes along the way. But each morning began spending time experiencing God's presence through worship. It became the place where I found peace, where I found guidance, and where I was able to connect my heart with God's so He could encourage and illuminate truth to me. It was a place of spiritual battle, sometimes wrestling with God with questions of why, how, and when. I found myself wondering when the next *episode* would present itself. Sometimes it was battle against the enemy who had taken over the mind of my wife leading her into a deep state of depression, being controlled by the torment of addiction. I was in a season where the valley couldn't seem to get any deeper.

I believe it was in God's presence during this time that my heart was protected. Later it would become a place of healing and forgiveness. It would evolve eventually into a place of joy as God restored me, renewed me, and afterward gave me a life that has been an incredible blessing personally and in ministry. *God restored me through being in His presence, and He can do the same for anyone who humbles themselves before Him.*

Three-Chord Willie

As a trained musician I have a deep appreciation and even admiration for a musician who displays virtuosic talent. I like classic rock, jazz, gospel music, contemporary Christian music, and pretty much any kind of music except music with violent or perverse lyrics. I'm pretty open-minded when it comes to musical style. I'm always willing to pause to listen to an exceptional musician.

But on a trip to Mariscala, Uruguay, in 2001 I met "Three-Chord Willie." That wasn't his real name. He didn't speak a lick of English, so our communication with each other was pretty limited. But I could tell he had a true heart for worship.

On the first night of the nightly meetings that we conducted for a week, I was scheduled to preach but had also brought my trumpet so was asked to sit in with the praise band. The instrumentation was somewhat unconventional and included an accordion player, hand drummer, some singers, and a guitar player (Three-Chord Willie). The accordion player was the leader of the group. She was pretty amazing musically but more so as a worship leader. By the way, we walked by her house every day while in that town and noticed a lamb tied out to a stake. We'd talk to the lamb as we walked by, sometimes petting it. On our last evening there we were invited to her house for dinner. When we walked up, the lamb was gone and only the rope tied to the stake remained. I'll let you figure out the rest of the story. He was delicious.

It became evident during the warm-up that Three-Chord Willie (TCW) only knew three chords...in one key. I was struggling to translate the keys being told to me in Spanish and the occasional shout-out of a chord here and there. What I began to notice, however, is that even though most of the time TCW was playing in a different key, he was worshiping. He was leading himself into the presence of God with those three chords, and it was rather miraculous. The musical aspect was not what you or I would call "good," but the spiritual aspect was of heavenly origin. He left an impression on me that leading from a place of God's presence is so important as we lead others.

I would add that there have been times that I've heard some musically "perfect" songs in a worship set that led nowhere. I'm not sure they even resonated beyond the roof of the building. This happens when we leave leading from His presence out of the worship-leading picture. Bring on the fantastic musicians, but make sure they practice the presence of God in their life, otherwise you'll end up with a performance that never gets past the outer court.

Always do everything you can to lead from a place of God's presence. There's no shame in stepping down from a praise team for a season to refocus on practicing the presence of God in your life and worship. Doing so will likely mean you'll return with a renewed passion for worship, which will benefit everyone and will bless God in a new way. I'm not talking about being flaky stepping on and off every couple of months. Church musicians are sometimes known for their flakiness, by the way. That is likely emotion-driven and not spirit-driven. I'm talking about taking time to renew your passion for worship. His presence must become everything you desire for yourself and others.

CHAPTER 6

∞∞

The World's Greatest Worship Leader

Worship Songs Versus Artist Songs

One of the distinct advantages in the United States that worship leaders have today is the prevalence of Christian radio stations. If you cruise up and down the FM dial in your vehicle, it's pretty likely you'll come across several gospel or contemporary Christian music radio stations. I thank God for them having been raised in the '70s when you could count on one hand the number of contemporary Christian artists around. I encourage you to support these stations with your prayers and resources. They have introduced millions to the latest songs, many of which you may end up doing in a worship set.

Because of the blessing of Christian radio, many of the people you lead are familiar with the songs you use to lead in worship before ever stepping foot through your church door. This makes the introduction of new songs much easier and more fruitful. However, you need to understand the difference between a worship song and an artist song.

An artist song sometimes tells a story, may have some quirkiness to it, and is likely never intended to lead people into a worship experience. They're intended to be observed and not used to invite. They are likely not written with the intention of people singing along. They honor God and maybe even inspire some soul-searching. They may bring a tear to your eye because of the story they tell. They are good and inspiring. However, they aren't intended to facilitate corporate worship. They're good to use for offertories, maybe even altar calls, but they don't fit into the tabernacle model very well. I won't list the names of songs for comparison or artists. Some artists write a mixture of artist songs and worship songs, which is awesome. Some focus on one or the other. That's okay too. It's pretty likely as they conceive the songs themselves that they have a clear objective as to the outcome of the song and its purpose.

Worship songs, however, often include words and phrases such as "I worship You," "We worship You," "You can," "You will," "You have," or lyrics which include attributes of God. Their lyrics and melodies are "singable," encouraging people to join in. They invite. They might celebrate who God is, what He's done, or what He's going to do. Some repeat a lot. Some are upbeat and celebratory. Others slow and worshipful, conceived to point people to God's presence.

Remember, the flow of the worship song set is purposeful for leading people into the holy of holies. I've been in worship settings where an artist song was inserted and the momentum of moving into God's presence was disrupted. Before the song, people were singing along, engaged, following where the leader was taking them, understanding the destination before they got there. The artist song began, and people stopped singing. Some even sat down after having been standing the entire time. The lyric was too difficult or the melody beyond their ability in some way. You can "recover," but it may be a challenge. Flow is important to keep people engaged in where you're taking them, so consider carefully how you use both worship songs and artist songs. The distinguishing between the two types is not an exact science, by the way. Perhaps a better rule of thumb would be that if the song engages your people and you feel it takes them where you're going, then use it. And please don't fall into the trap of using it just because your praise team likes jamming to it. If that's the case, then consider using it for an offertory or call to worship type of song, maybe as people leave giving them an encouraging send-off.

Worship should be linear as it leads to God's presence. By linear worship I mean that spiritually and musically we're thinking in terms of flow and direction. Each song melding into the next to create a line without segments from the outer court to the holy of holies. One song transitioning into the next as if each blended together to create one song of worship is the key to linear worship. When we begin to think of worship as one song after another, it affects the flow and the transitions of one song to the next. Think of the set as one unit that takes us from the outer court to the holy of holies.

Where Is the World's Greatest Worship Leader?

Over the years, as contemporary forms of worship have grown in prominence in worship settings, I've been asked many times who I believe the *best* or *greatest* worship leader is. I suppose this sort of question has come about because of the readily available recordings, videos, worship concerts, and Christian radio. In some ways it feels like a secular question and not a spiritual one. But the truth is that many formerly secular modes of sharing music have been utilized to expand the reach of all sorts of worship music styles. I think it's great yet has some drawbacks.

One of those drawbacks is that the industry has become just that—an industry, one that is concerned with profit. Some may argue not necessarily only profit, but it is without question an aspect of the industry. This has become an attraction for some worship musicians whose motivation may be less than spiritual. We know that the love of money can corrupt (1 Timothy 6:10) making temptation plausible.

I'm reminded of an audition I had at a well-known theme park back in the early '80s. I was having a great day at the theme park with a buddy from college. We stopped into a gospel show to listen. I had just rededicated my life to Jesus, and the familiar tunes from my childhood brought back some great memories of times I would sit at the piano and play hymns out of a hymnal or try to figure out a song by ear that I had heard on an album. At the end of the group's set they announced they were looking for a new piano player because their current one was moving on to another gig of some kind. I perked up and seized the moment by going up to the bandleader right after the last note. We talked for a while. I explained I was from out of state, and he offered me an audition right on the spot. Wow! Talk about exciting! Thoughts of grandeur began to run through my head, thoughts about dropping out of college to pursue a new avenue for my music skill, thoughts of how much would I make. All of these were pragmatic and realistic thoughts, but none was really that spiritual. Shame on me!

But as we made our way in the back areas of the theme park to a studio for the audition, the guy who had been singing praises to God only moments before regaled me with stories of his sexual exploits with "that one," "that girl over there," etc. I quickly realized that he was in it for the business, but not for the ministry. I wasn't even sure if he was actually a Christ-follower. Perhaps he is now and is using his talents to serve Jesus powerfully. I hope so. I didn't get the gig, which was no surprise. I didn't have the ability to play by ear then that I do now. I trusted that it was all part of God's bigger plan for my life by being passed over. God will use many experiences in our life to grow us and lead us where He wants us to go.

I say all of this to say that I have this belief that the *greatest* or *best* worship leader in the world is someone few people have even heard of. It's probably some incredibly devoted worship leader who serves a small church in a place that most people have never heard of. The best worship leaders are committed to living a life of holiness. They show up faithfully each week to lead people into the presence of God, and it's an outflow of their deep devotion to the kingdom and their love for Jesus. They have an anointing that could easily be exploited if *discovered*, but they're content to lead the people to which they've been called. Maybe it's you who is reading this right now. Chances are whoever it is doesn't even realize it. That speaks to their humility.

This is a reminder that leading worship is not a competition. We should all seek God's anointing when we lead worship and come before Him humbly with our sincere offering of praise and thanksgiving. If it becomes a competition, it won't be long before it becomes a performance. We might as well be playing secular music because the sacredness of our role will vanish. Whether you lead in a big or small church makes no difference in the eyes of God. Your heart of worship does. *Seek the anointing each time you lead.*

CHAPTER 7

<><><><><><><><><><><><><><><><><><><><><><><><><><><><><><><><><><><><><><><><><><>

Seeking the Anointing

What Is Anointing?

The Bible is full of references to anointing oil. We see them mostly in
the Old Testament. There is, however, the use of the word *anointing*
in the New Testament that is not in conjunction with oil.

In the Old Testament we see the Hebrew word for anointing,
mishcah. This word has a meaning of a gift used in times of conse-
cration. We see it used this way at the anointing of King David (1
Samuel 16:12–14) and in other passages describing the tabernacle.
You could fill a book with a study of anointing oil's use in the Old
Testament, and if you have a heart to write it, you have my encouragement to do so. I would most certainly read it.

The use of anointing oil in the Old Testament has a sacredness
that we should recognize because it is a type of forerunner to the
anointing in the New Testament. It suffices to say that when anointing oil was used in the Old Testament it wasn't an insignificant act
and should be viewed as sacred in that context and in the context
of worship. Because of its many uses in the tabernacle and later the
temple, it's safe to say it has a worship connotation.

Many Messianic Jewish teachers consider oil a symbol of the
Holy Spirit. The lamps in the holy place, for example, are a representation of the Holy Spirit not only because of the flame, but also
because of the oil used in them. If we equate the Holy Spirit with any

use of oil in the Old Testament the majority of the time seems to be an appropriate equation.

However, as we move into the New Testament we see in some places the stand-alone use of the word *anointing*. The Greek word for this is *chrisma*, and it's meaning is important for any worship leader or worship musician to grasp. Once I understood this concept or truth, it changed the way I led worship and my understanding of worship's sacredness.

The meaning of the word is "special endowment of the Holy Spirit." Let that sink into your brain and your spirit for a moment. (Example: 1 John 2:27.)

When I was a worship pastor at a church in the Chicago area, the bass player in our band shared a story with me that I've never forgotten. He had played in several gospel groups, and now I was pushing him in his adapting to playing contemporary praise and worship. He was a good sport, patient, and committed. He adapted very well musically, but he most importantly brought a spiritual maturity to the group that was a blessing.

He shared with me that his gospel group played at a festival of some kind many years ago, and there were other gospel groups there that he considered much better musically. After his group had played, one of the other groups came up to them behind the stage and inquired about how powerful their *performance* was and how people responded. They recognized there was something different about them. It was the anointing. The other groups, though musically skilled and sincere, lacked the anointing of the Holy Spirit that led people into the presence of God. I can only hope that the other groups learned a valuable lesson from that experience and began to seek the anointing when they ministered. If they did, then I'm confident they moved from a place of performance to a place of anointing.

The bass player that shared this story wasn't bragging. In fact, he was eager to share that his group wasn't nearly as good musically as the others. He was a humble servant who offered his musical gifts back to the Lord and sought after, desired, craved the anointing.

When you lead worship, and I mean every time you lead worship, do you seek the anointing (chrisma)of the Holy Spirit? If not, then now is the time to begin this holy habit. Why would we want to minister without the anointing, the blessing of the Holy Spirit, the presence of the Holy Spirit? If we aren't seeking the anointing as we lead, then we're really settling for second best. That's not "my utmost" for His highest.

Back to that anointing oil idea from the Old Testament. The oil used for anointing was fragrant. It was thick. When it was applied, the aroma lingered in the air for the people to take in through the nose and find pleasure in it. As we lead worship, let's seek the anointing and let's pray that the people we lead would sense the presence of the Holy Spirit, His aroma, His fragrance, and His lingering in their lives. The anointing counteracts a performance mind-set and spirit.

Tabernacle in Heaven

There's a key passage of Scripture that contributes to my philosophy of the worship continuum. It's found in a book in the New Testament that has no attributed author. There are many speculations about who wrote the book of Hebrews, and it's quite clear that the author was familiar with the life that surrounded the temple and the worship of the people of God. They seem to have some very specific insight into the structure of the temple and the symbolism of the normal activity of the center of culture at the time. Consider these words found in Hebrews 8:1–6:

> Now the main point of what we are saying is this: We do have such a high priest, who sat down at the right hand of the throne of the Majesty in heaven, and who serves in the sanctuary, the true tabernacle set up by the Lord, not by a mere human being.
>
> Every high priest is appointed to offer both gifts and sacrifices, and so it was necessary for this one also to have something to offer. If he were on earth, he would not be a priest, for there

are already priests who offer the gifts prescribed by the law. They serve at a sanctuary that is a copy and shadow of what is in heaven. This is why Moses was warned when he was about to build the tabernacle: "See to it that you make everything according to the pattern shown you on the mountain." But in fact the ministry Jesus has received is as superior to theirs as the covenant of which he is mediator is superior to the old one, since the new covenant is established on better promises. (Hebrews 8:1–6 NIV)

We first have to recognize that the high priest referred to here is Jesus Himself and the location is in heaven. Jesus served in no practical role in the earthly temple of His day. That was relegated to mortals whose roles were firmly established through tradition. The writer refers to the *true tabernacle*, a heavenly tabernacle.

The author goes on to describe the earthly tabernacle and temple as "a copy and shadow of what is in heaven." Did you catch that? Moses was commanded with very specific instructions on the building of the tabernacle, but even as specific and particular as these instructions were, they were but a shadow of the real thing in heaven.

You also get a sense that as the author mentions the new covenant that comes through Jesus as a better thing, so, too, is the tabernacle in heaven a better thing than the earthly tabernacle or temple. The earthly tabernacle falls short of the glory of the one in heaven. Clearly there is a tabernacle in heaven and any earthly emulation is lacking in some way.

Consider this then. If there's a tabernacle in heaven, and Scripture is clear that there is, then worship must happen continually as far back as time and as far forward as eternity, as well as in the present moment.

In Luke 15 we see three parables about the lost being found. The first two that we see have an intersection with heaven. The parable of the lost coin (Luke 15:8–10) and the parable of the lost sheep (Luke 15:1–7) have similar ending statements. They both indicate that when a sinner repents, there is rejoicing in heaven. In one case it's angels that rejoice, and in the other it's not stated who, but someone or something rejoices in the presence of God! Heaven and earth intersect, and rejoicing ensues. Something that happens on earth is celebrated in heaven. Why? Because there's a continuum of worship in heaven that has had no beginning and will have no end!

So if heaven and earth can intersect when a sinner repents, why can't they intersect when we worship? I believe they can and do. When we begin to understand that our leading of worship is connected to the worship continuum in heaven, it brings us to a deeper understanding of the sacredness of leading people in worship. We take the hand of God and the hand of the people. We bring them together and step out of the way so that God can transform hearts, minds, and lives. This is a picture of joining our earthly worship with the worship continuum in heaven. To connect people to God in worship is supernatural and is aided by the Holy Spirit's anointing.

You and I are invited to be part of the worship continuum. God desires it for us, and that's pretty amazing stuff!

CONCLUSION

◇◇

It was a cold, dreary winter day in Toledo, Ohio. I had created a space for a simplistic recording studio with a digital piano, mic, and cassette recorder. It was actually in what must have once been a place for storing canned goods in the basement of the 1928 Tudor-style home we lived in at the time. The space was only six feet by six feet with just enough room for me to squeeze behind the keyboard and sit on the bench. I would often close the doors and lose myself in worship. God had been dealing with me about a change that was coming. It was not yet well defined but would come into focus in a miraculous way in that little room. On this particular day I wasn't expecting it, but God spoke to me about the new trajectory of my life. As I worshiped I felt the Spirit tell me that doors would open for me to become a worship leader. Up to this point I'd been on a worship team playing trumpet and doing some arranging, but things were about to change. As I sang "I Exalt Thee," the little room filled with the presence of God and the confirmation that I had been seeking was given. It was one of the most powerful sensations of His presence that I've ever experienced. After this, doors started miraculously opening for me to move into my first full-time worship pastor role. Things would never be the same. *I* would never be the same. To this day I can't lead "I Exalt Thee" without weeping and remembering that moment. I had experienced the worship continuum for the first time.

I set out to write this small book in January 2020 as part of my yearly goals and at what I believe was the leading of the Holy Spirit. I'd talked about it a lot and bounced the idea off of a few trusted friends. Little did I know that shortly after I began putting my fingers to the keyboard, a pandemic would break out in our world through

COVID-19. This was added to the chaos of the political climate that had arisen over the past few years. Along came social unrest, riots, and protests. Our country seemed to become a perfect storm of rising anger, conspiracy theories, and other signs of Jesus's soon return.

I can think of no better time for us to worship the only one who truly has answers for the times in which we live. If our hope is in the world, then we're going to be sadly disappointed by what the world offers. However, if our hope is in Jesus Christ we know the security of our eternity. We know that we are moving closer to living in the worship continuum in heaven. It's going to be glorious. It's going to solve a lot of the temporal issues with which we currently struggle. It's going to be eternal. Why not aim to experience as much of it now, here, as we seek the anointing each time we lead ourselves and others in worship?

It's my hope that you will pass on this concept to others and that they, too, will experience the intersection of heaven and earth through worship that is strongly connected to the worship continuum. Whether that connection be experienced in a worship service with thousands or in a tiny little root cellar alone, I'm confident it will change you and foster your passion for worshiping our God. Blessings to you on your worship journey!

DISCUSSION QUESTIONS

Chapter 1

1. Do you have an accountability partner or group who can help you remain humble as you serve God in ministry?
2. How do you apply worship and prayer in your life? If you don't currently, how can you begin?
3. Do you understand the power against the enemy that comes through praise and worship? How does this apply individually and corporately?

Chapter 2

1. Have you ever experienced anything like "the heavenly chorus" or the account at the Uruguay Youth Camp? If so, how would you explain it?
2. Do you believe it's possible for you to experience something like the heavenly chorus or the Uruguay Youth Camp experience in your local church?
3. Do you believe that prayer is the foundation of revival?

Chapter 3

1. Do you agree that we can bring "strange fire" before God today?
2. Are there changes in your lifestyle that you could make to bring more glory to God?

3. How might you enhance your commitment to your praise team or your role in ministry?

Chapter 4

1. Have you considered how utilizing the "tabernacle progression" might influence the way you lead and participate in the personal and congregational worship setting?
2. Are there ways you can foster going deeper in personal worship so that you might lead others deeper in worship?
3. What things might you add to the way you prepare to lead in worship so that you can take people with you into God's presence?

Chapter 5

1. Do you seek God's presence when you worship personally and/or corporately?
2. If not, how can you make changes that would help you strive to lead in such a way that people would be more aware of God's presence?
3. Do you truly desire to see people come into God's presence in worship, or are you satisfied with only you doing so?

Chapter 6

1. Do you have a good understanding of the difference between a worship song and an artist song?
2. How might you use this understanding in planning the music for a worship service or worship event?
3. How do you guard against viewing worship as a competition of some kind?

Chapter 7

1. In what ways can you seek the *chrismal* anointing as you lead worship or participate on a praise team?
2. Is it possible to experience the anointing each time you lead or worship?
3. Can the anointing affect the way you lead people into God's presence in worship?

ABOUT THE AUTHOR

Gordon has served as a worship pastor at churches in Ohio, Illinois, Colorado, and Kansas. Gordon's interest in music began at a young age through piano lessons, then later he took an interest in the trumpet. Learning to play several instruments on his own, he chose to major in music in undergrad and graduate schools with emphasis on music composition. An encounter with the Holy Spirit led him to accept the call into full-time ministry after a career in education and as a freelance professional musician. Gordon has written several praise and worship songs during his time in ministry, some holding copyrights with the Library of Congress. His ministry has been marked by the development of worshipers' musical skill and praise team development, but most importantly marked by the fostering of people's passion for worshiping God in spirit and in truth. Gordon currently serves as lead pastor of Emmanuel Church in Abilene, Kansas, a non-denominational church that seeks to honor God through sharing the love, grace, worship, and truth of Jesus Christ. He's married to Amy, a worship leader, and they have three adult daughters. Gordon is an avid hunter and enjoys working on restorations of old cars in his spare time.

CPSIA information can be obtained
at www.ICGtesting.com
Printed in the USA
LVHW041352051121
702522LV00001B/44